GOD HAS NOT FORGOTTEN YOU!

Oyin Oladipo

GOD HAS NOT FORGOTTEN YOU!

ISBN-13: 978-1537496375

ISBN-10: 1537496379

DEDICATION

I dedicate this book to the person who introduced
God to me and taught me that God will never forget
me.
My mother

Mrs Victoria Ebun Abitogun

Thank you, mummy.

INTRODUCTION

The title of this book is a bold declaration in a world that has more questions than answers.

The reality of everyday life is that we experience less of life's pleasantries than we would love to. There is a desire in all of us to partake daily out of the promises that God made to us in the Bible.

I started my Christian journey with a very high expectation of all God's promises being fulfilled in my life as and when I needed them to be. To my disdain, life happened and God did not show up to deliver me as I thought He would. My conclusion bordered loosely on the assumptions that either God did not exist or He had forgotten me.

Deep within me and from the things I had seen, I knew and accepted that God existed. This left me with my second assumption that God had forgotten or rejected me. My sins stared me in the face and if God knew them all, then it made sense for Him to reject or forget about me.

I have not written this book because I have all the answers. No -I wrote it whilst on a quest to find answers to some of my questions and feelings.

I hope that some of the answers I have found and written here will help you in your own journey too. I pray that in this book you will come to understand that God has not forgotten you and that your faith in Him will be firmly established.

I wish that life had no storms and that we constantly feel God's presence with us. Afterall, the Bible tells us that God is always with us His Children. My dilemma has been how to reconcile what is written in the Bible with my daily post-modern experience (and that is what this book is all about).

Although I cannot guarantee that all your questions will be answered, I can guarantee that this book will open your mind to the possibility and reality of God's love and favour. As much as I am known for making people laugh, I cannot promise that you'll laugh out loud whilst reading it, but I can guarantee a few smiles here and there. Above all, I pray that your mind will be enlightened and that you will see God in a better light - that He will never leave His beloved.

Oyinlade Oladipo
Feb 8, 2017
London, United Kingdom

TABLE OF CONTENTS

Isaiah 49: 15 & 16.

'Can a mother forget the infant at her breast,
walk away from the baby she bore?
But even if mothers forget,
I'd never forget you—never.
Look, I've written your names on the backs of my
hands.'
Message Bible. Emphasis added

'[And the Lord answered] Can a woman forget her
nursing child, that she should not have compassion
on the son of her womb? Yes, they may forget,
yet I will not forget you.
Behold, I have indelibly imprinted (tattooed a
picture of) you on the palm of each of My hands; [O
Zion] your walls are continually before Me.'
The Amplified Bible. Emphasis added

Oyin Oladipo

1.
FEEL FORGOTTEN?

On a bright summer day, there is no better place to be than at a Carnival. Children are having fun jumping on bouncy castles and trampolines, burning calories to the delight of the ice cream vendor who magically never runs out of supplies. Oblivious to the world around them, lovers hold hands whispering sweet nothings into each other's ears. Melodious music from the brass band caress ears setting feet dancing and bodies twisting. Across the field the stand-up comedian is in his elements as he tells stories that have them all in fits of laughter. It can be said that the sun came out in all its splendour to make the day a memorable one. Sweating under the heat of the sun, Dave can hardly keep up with the orders coming in for his special barbecued chicken. The crowd, the pull and push, the fun, there is indeed no better place to be on this day.

But wait a minute, who is that lone figure crying in the midst of all the laughter at the comedy stand? Standing right there in the happy crowd is none other than little Sarah sobbing profusely, no one pays her any serious attention. *"Mama, watch that child"*, the comedian bellows into the microphone, setting everyone off in a bout of laughter. Gasping for breath, Sarah makes her way through the crowd, shivering and shaking, too frightened to utter a word., She feared what in her little mind was the worst that can happen; her minder has forgotten to collect her, she is lost!

Have you ever been forgotten? Lost in a foreign town? Not called for the interview of a lifetime because your name was missed out on the shortlist? Perhaps you are in prison and the people you consider friends refuse to contact you. The list can go on and on. But worse than them all is when you have that feeling (that I do have at times) of being forgotten by God Himself. It is a scary thought; one that we all fear and pray not to experience, but it remains a fact of life that there are those times that we feel forgotten by God Almighty.

David felt like that when King Saul chased after him and wanted to kill him. A humble shepherd boy, David was going about his day job tending his father's sheep when one day Samuel the prophet came and permanently changed the course of his life. He never asked to be famous and had already become notorious in the neighbourhood as the senseless lad who boasted of attacking a lion with his bare hands. He was the black sheep of his family, the product of a possible affair between Jesse and a lady whose name was not known (rumour had it that she was a prostitute).

It was to this rather shy, reserved, ordinary shepherd boy that Samuel came and anointed King over Israel. Samuel said that it was God's Will and no one in their right mind would challenge this wise man (King Saul did and all in the land knew what happened to him). David was left with no choice than to accept Samuel's action as God's Will indeed, and he waited for the day that he would sit on the throne over the twelve tribes. Time dragged on for over twenty years yet the anointed king did not mount the throne. He became a General in Saul's army after killing Goliath and thereafter was a period of being a part of the aristocracy; but most of those twenty years were spent as a fugitive after he fell out of favour with the King. We read in the Psalms that David wrote of how it seemed that God, his God had abandoned him. Things degenerated so much that at a point he had to feign madness in order to escape death from a pagan king. It seemed as if God has forgotten His own anointed!

It is easy for preachers to paint a picture of a God who is as present as the neighbours we see daily. But it is a rather different picture that reality presents to me in everyday life. Many countries have systems in place to put leaders in check and ensure that they deliver on their promises. Under certain circumstances, Parliamentarians can be called to order or recalled by their constituents if they forget the people they are in office to represent. But who calls God to order when He appears to forget me?

"If God does not help me then who will?" a man of faith might cry in desperation. Kate, a tutor at Oakington Immigration Removal Centre, Cambridgeshire once told me "I don't believe in an intervening God". Like her, there are many who say that God is no longer interested in the affairs of this world. Atheists take it even further and state as a matter of fact that there is no God. At times, I'm tempted to agree with both the deist and the atheist. When I think of my married friends who despite all they have done still have not conceived for years, a colleague's mum who died from leukaemia, the many who lost their lives in natural disasters, the baby born HIV positive, the innocent people who died at the hand of suicide bombers, the many devout Christians who live in poverty and

have become the forgotten peoples of the earth or of a person in detention in some remote country without the hope of release. If we are to look critically at the happenings around us, I am afraid we might feel that God does not have us in mind as much as the Bible says He does.

But there are times when God does burst into our everyday lives and work miracles. His actions are as explosive and colourful as fireworks, as He gives a cure here and a healing there. And in certain cases dead people have been miraculously brought back to life after prayers to God. However, seeing a crippled man carried home still crippled at a Reinhard Bonkke Gospel Campaign held in Akure, Nigeria in 2003 got me seriously worried. Many people at that event were healed and blessed but why was this one not healed? Miracles do happen, but they seem to be the exception rather than the rule. How I wish that they were as constant as the oxygen I breathe, that I could be as sure of them as I was of my pay at the end of the month as a housing officer at Westminster Council, London. Does God still care, does He remember, is He active or has He gone off to sleep and left this world (of which I am part of) to its fate?

I write not as one who has seen, and met God like St John, or like priests and preachers who claim to commune daily with God on an almost *face to face* basis. I write as a lay man who like the rest of humanity seeks God and searches for answers to life's questions.

Daily, the hearts of men cry for a higher power to intervene in their cases. "My God, My God, why hast thou forsaken me?" [1] was a normal Jewish cry made famous by God's Son Himself - Jesus Christ our Lord. Deep within me, I rejoice that Jesus knows what it is like to feel forsaken by our Almighty Father.

As good as it sounds, knowing that Jesus understands what it means to be forsaken by God would not have made much difference if like every other man, He had died and remained in the grave overcome by death.

However, from the dark cloud that accompanied that famous shout at Calvary came the burst of sunlight of the resurrection. The disciples who thought they had been abandoned by Jesus realised at the resurrection that they were no longer going to be alone. Jesus promised to be with them always. He had become in the words of

Hebrews 4:15 *"a high priest which can be touched with the feeling of our infirmities".*[2]

If that then means that the same Jesus that was forsaken by God is now with God in heaven pleading for us, then we have hope. There, standing beside the Father is someone like us. A man who drums daily into our Father's ear the fact that Oyin is in need of help, that Sally needs healing, that Zainab is in trouble.

Does God forget His children? When we look at happenings around us we might be inclined to think that He does. The Bible also, in certain passages appears to give mixed messages that sometimes God does forget His children, and at other times remembers them. Passages like "and God remembered Noah..."[3] if taken at face value can suggest that God can forget, for there will be no need to *remember* where the ability to *forget* does not exist. I have heard preachers encourage people to cry out to God for remembrance. And sprinkled all over the Old Testament are passages like "remember me O Lord". All these suggest that God can at times forget His people.

If God does forget us, I submit then that we are in deep trouble. A deity, an almighty one, who suffers from memory lapses, is not worthy to be called

God. If Christianity's God does not hold each of His children in His mind every second of the day, then I greatly fear that men like Richard Dawkins would be proven right - that we are deluded.

But does YHWH the God of Abraham forget His own people? Does God forget you? Let's look into the Bible for an answer to this question. Please bear with me if we have to proceed slowly and steadily. We are embarking on a journey that is more like a marathon and not a sprint. I hope that when you have finished reading this book, your faith in the character and person of God will be so strong that you will be immoveable, because you would have come to the understanding that no matter what, you have a God that never forgets you. Your God is indeed an ever present help in times of trouble.

REFERENCES

1. Mark 15:34, Psalms 22:1

2. Hebrews 4:15 Paraphrased by author.

   Full text reads thus in the NIV:

   "For we do not have a high priest who is unable to empathize with our weaknesses, but we have one who has been tempted in every way, just as we are—yet he did not sin".

3. Genesis 8:1.

Remember in this context means 'called to mind' or 'thought of'

2.

GOD IS NOT A MAN.

God is not a deceiver that He should offer to support us, and then, when we lean upon Him, should slip away from us.

\- St Augustine

He was a student at the University of Texas at about the same time Alex Hayley did the research for the movie, Roots. That probably spurred in him the desire to pass on to his offspring the story of his own roots. My father, Oladipo was a great storyteller. Since he passed on ten years ago, I have not met anyone else who has such a good command of my family history.

Not only did he tell stories of the feats performed by my great-grandfather, he told stories of the generation that existed when the earliest Europeans set foot on our soil. Tales that sounded too incredible to be true, of how his own great grandmother was kidnapped as a little girl and sold as a slave, not to the Europeans but to an African warlord. How by mere chance as an adult she met some strangers at a market and through what resembled a Hollywood escape plot they took her back to her family village hundreds of miles away. I wish I could tell you how many days they spent navigating through jungles and forest but sadly, I do not have that information.

He recounted these stories as if he experienced them himself. If I had watched Dr Who as a child, I would have thought that Oladipo borrowed the TARDIS and went back in time.

A walking history book with a clever brain, he never ceased to let me know where my ancestors came from and the great feats done by those whose bloods run in my veins.

I must confess that at that time, I did not see the point of such old stories, but now I know why my father took his time to relate to me my family history. By reading the ink stains on the sheet of yester-years, I will take up the challenge of the sages in my lineage and forge for myself a noble path.

In our quest to understand who God is, the first thing we need to establish is not His history but His nature and character all through our history. If there is anything that God desires, it is for His people to know Him. "Those that know their God shall be strong", [1] Daniel was told. Strength and power (the ability to make things happen) come

11

from knowledge. As my Dad would probably say, "if you don't know who you are, you will live a life void of purpose and strength". Anyone who desires to live the life that God has called him to live needs to equip himself with the knowledge of God.

The Bible is silent about the 'origin' of God. The first words of the world's most famous Bible, the Authorised Version are "In the beginning, God...".[2] We see Him as being present from the beginning. It was not His beginning. It was the beginning of creation, our beginning. We know from studying the Bible that He existed from what in our limited mind we call eternity past. There is no time in God's 'timeline'; in fact He has no timeline. He just is. This blows my mind and makes me stand in awe of Him. I am a product of my parents; I know where I came from. Without my Dad, Oladipo and Mum, Victoria I would not exist. In the same way without Daniel and Regina (my maternal grandparents), there would be no Victoria and consequently no Oyin. A good genealogist can trace my lineage back through my ancestors just like in the BBC program *Who Do You Think You Are?* But God has no predecessor. He is God, self-sufficient, everlasting. He is not a part of our species. He is in a class of His own, the theological term for that is "He is Holy".

Man was made in God's image, but sadly, present day man is not a true reflection of God. After the fall, Adam retained his physical form, but lost God's essence in him; he became sinful. Therefore, man cannot truly represent God. To know the character and nature of God, we must look beyond man. Over the years, we have tried to describe who God is and what He can do using man as the yardstick. But God is not man. "God is not a man that he should lie",[3] says the scriptures. We limit God when we refuse to see Him as The Almighty.

Who then is God? As I was about to type the answer to this I paused for a few minutes, at a loss at how to describe God. I had known about Him from childhood but I cannot say that I or anyone else really know Him as we should "For now we see only a reflection as in a mirror; then we shall see face to face. Now I know in part; then I shall know fully, even as I am fully known" 1 Corinthians 13:12. NIV

I might not know all that God is, but I know what He is not! He is not a man! Unlike man, God is capable of doing what He says He will do. He is Perfect. Imagine a state where everything is all positive, where there is no sorrow, heartache, fear, disappointment, distortions, diseases. Imagine a state of purity, love, kindness, hope, bliss, tranquillity, positive exuberance, acceptance and truth - that state my friend is just a fraction of who God is. The Bible says "God is Love"[4]. God does not just carry out the act of loving, He is Love. With Him, loving is not an ability, He is love Himself. When you love, you show and demonstrate something of His very being. The Bible shouts out His attributes, Nature- His canvass, rolls out His praises and tells of the wondrous things He has done. But who is God? How can I know Him? The answer to this question is found in the one person who loved perfectly, Jesus; God revealed in human form.

As Jesus said in John 10:30 "I and the Father are One". Jesus laid claim to being God and those who truly know Him will believe it.

John 1:1 puts it this way: "In the beginning was the Word, and the Word was with God and the Word was God". Later on in the same account told by John, the Word was revealed as Jesus, Mary's son. Notice the phrase "and the Word was God" Jesus is God. Therefore if we want to know who God is, we look at Jesus. If we want to determine God's character, we simply need to look at the character of the Man who the Bible says is the express image of God the Father - Jesus Christ.

God is not a man in that He is not limited by the things that limit the ordinary man. He does not possess the anti-God nature of the common man. Yet here lies a great mystery! In saving man, God became human, was born and named Jesus. He is therefore a man in that sense, but not a sinful man. He is perfect, the perfect Man. Oh what a joy, God becoming man in order to save man!

If Jesus stood before you today, would you believe what He says? Here is a Man who no one can fault; even those who don't agree that He is God's Son still affirm that He is a righteous Man. In Him is no lie. He is trustworthy. It is Jesus who gives us a clear understanding of the nature of God. The good news for us here is that God is no longer distant and 'unknowable' "the word was made flesh and dwelt among us"[5]. God is with us in Jesus.

If despite all His might, God dwells only in and focuses on Heaven then we are doomed. He might easily forget us and not understand what it means to be human. Like the mythological gods on Mount Olympus, He may regard us as mere pawns in His hands, objects to be tossed to and fro to the delight of Zeus and his contemporaries. But in

15

Jesus, God became man, experienced and is still experiencing what it means to be a human being. He cannot forget us; <u>He is one of us</u>!

Many people followed Jesus during His days on earth. In the crowd were men and women who were with Him not only because of the miracles He performed, but to learn from Him. They were His disciples. From this group, He chose twelve men and called them Apostles, His right hand men. Of the twelve, about four were fishermen, one a tax collector, another one a religious militant and so on. These men were engaged in one form of employment or another prior to meeting this itinerant preacher, but all left their jobs to travel with him. The demand of working with Jesus was such that you could not combine it with any other thing. But while they were with Jesus, their sincere needs were always met.

Throughout His earthly life and ministry, Jesus showed to the world what it meant to be good. He showed compassion to the weak and gave hope to those in despair. A woman who was caught in adultery was forgiven by Him and told to go and sin no more. He raised Lazarus and others from the dead. He brought joy to the sorrowful. Many who came to Him with frowns on their faces left with beams of joy, except the religious leaders who came to test Him and those who lacked faith (such as the rich man told by Jesus to go and sell all that he had). Mothers trusted Him so much that they brought their children to be blessed by Him. Prostitutes met Him and had their lives transformed. Lepers were societal outcasts in Jesus' days; no one was allowed to have any physical contact with them. But in curing one, Jesus not only spoke the word of healing, He did the unimaginable, He touched Him!

To Jesus, everyone was important. Sinners became saints after encountering Him. This Man was an epitome of perfection, God's gift to the world. Sinless, yet He loved sinners. On the cross, He carried our sins. He experienced the worst of human nature. He became sin and was punished for us. When we sin, we no longer fear God's wrath because we have seen His willingness to forgive in the drama that unfolded at Golgotha. Instead we are shown love and mercy. It is this Christ that we are called to trust.

Tell me then. How can such a One who showed so much compassion to us turn around and forget us now? Is God subject to the forgetfulness we all experience as humans? No! Forgetting or loss of memory is not a strength but a weakness. And the Almighty God is not weak, He is not mortal man!

By His nature as seen in the Old Testament and exemplified by Jesus, God is not one to forget His people. Banish the thought from your mind that God can forget you. I have quoted Isaiah 49:15 at the start of this book because it clearly tells us that God cannot forget us. He remembers what you told Him seventy years ago. Your prayers are before Him and in His time, everything will work out.

Isaiah gives us an almost impossible situation, that of a mother forgetting her infant child. The bond between a mother and her child is one of the strongest on earth, it transcends human reasoning. God puts His claim against and over this relationship. He says even if the impossible happens, and the strongest of all human relationships get broken, He will not break His own rule.

The Amplified Bible expresses Isaiah 49:16 in a remarkable way, I *have indelibly imprinted (tattooed a picture of) you on the palm of each of my   hands.*
The parts of our body that we see the most are the palms of our hands. We also use them more than many other body parts. If anything goes wrong

with the hand, we are quick to notice it. The Amplified Bible says that not only are we in God's palms, we are tattooed on them. People tattoo the names and images of loved ones on body parts as a permanent reminder. God has got us permanently imprinted on the palms of His hands. He cannot forget us! This should put an end to all arguments. God is telling you what He told ancient Israel, 'I am thinking about you'. You are engraved in the palm of God's hands. You are constantly before Him. He can never forget you, no not ever!

GOD CAN CHOOSE NOT TO REMEMBER

Can God's memory fail Him? No! Does God's memory fail Him? No! But He can choose not to remember.

'For I will forgive their wickedness and will remember their sins no more.' Jeremiah 31:34

God's memory does not fail Him, but He can choose not to remember some things any more. He can choose not to consider an issue, a person, an incident any more. In the passage above, God is specific about what He will not consider or remember anymore; our sins. This ability of His does not place a limit on Him; instead it is a manifestation of His power, only He has the ultimate will power.

No matter how hard a man tries to put an issue behind him for good, there will still be times when he will experience flashbacks. Man cannot completely choose not to remember. But God can choose to completely not consider an issue and not have flashbacks, He is that powerful!

Just as He can choose not to remember our sins anymore, God in His sovereignty can choose not to consider a person any more. How pathetic is the fellow whom God has chosen not to think of. I find no words to describe his fate. If he lives, he will go through life like a guinea pig in the devil's lab, subjected to all forms of ills that man can think of. An object of destruction who himself is on his way to everlasting damnation. May you never come across such a fellow and may that fellow not be you.

How can you be sure the pathetic fellow just described above won't be you? It is because you are tattooed on the palms of God's hands. You live in the hollow of His hands. According to Psalms 91, you dwell in His secret place, in His bedroom so to speak.

But how can you be sure that you are tattooed on

the palms of His hands? God remembered you whilst you were still a sinner and sent Jesus to die for you. Now that you are His child, He will not forget you. Paul says God "has given us a place beside Christ in heaven"[6].

You are engraved as lines on God's palms, you dwell in His secret place, and you are sitting with Him. He is considering you for good.

David says "what is man that you are mindful of him?" [7] God is mindful of you. He has His mind full of you. When a boy is in love with a girl, he constantly thinks of her, mentions her name subconsciously, talks about her, wants to be with her, and in most cases gets married to her. Lovers are never out of each other's minds. God is in love with you and is always thinking about you. Say it; God is in love with me and He is always thinking about   me.
Our relationship with Him is not only a parental one; it is also a love affair. Solomon says in his songs: *His banner over me is Love*[8]

"Who shall separate us from the Love of God?"[9], asked Paul. His answer was; nothing and no one! God loves you and as a result He is constantly thinking about you, He will not forget you. He knows your pains and as you will see in subsequent chapters, He has got everything under control and well planned. God is not a man to forget you or break His promises to you; He is not limited by what limits men. He is the Almighty One and you can trust Him

RECAP

- God is not a carnal man, he does not possess man's weak nature

- Jesus is God and in His days on earth, He cared for His people

- You are constantly in God's view: tattooed on His palms.

- God can choose not to remember anything-He does for our sins (He chooses not to remember our sins)

- God has chosen not to forget you, His child

- The relationship between God and us is not only as parent to child, it is also a love relationship.

God cannot and does not compromise His character, you can trust Him.

REFERENCES

1. Daniel 11:32

2. Genesis 1:1

3. Numbers 23:19

4. 1 John 4:8

5. John 1:14

6. Ephesians 2:6. Contemporary English Version

7. Psalms 8:4

8. Song of Solomon 2:4

9. Romans 8:35

3.
AND GOD REMEMBERED...

'You need not cry very loud; he is nearer to us than we think.'

- Brother Lawrence (1614 – 12 February 1691)

The Daily Mail of the 24 August 2012 carried the following sad story:

A mother has been arrested after she left her 15-month-old baby son in the back of her SUV and he boiled alive in 140F heat.

Concepcion Rodriguez, 26, unloaded six other children from the motor car when she arrived home from a store on Wednesday afternoon but forgot Benny Jnr.

He perished in a baby seat on the driveway outside their home in Corpus Christi, Texas, as outside temperatures reached 100F - making the heat inside the vehicle 140F.

Mrs Rodriguez only remembered about the child when her husband, 30, returned from work three hours later and asked where he was.

They found Benny unresponsive and rang an ambulance. Paramedics battled to revive the toddler but he was pronounced dead.[1]

When I was about to start writing this chapter I did a quick search in Google for cases of mothers forgetting their children. To my dismay I saw stories upon stories of mothers, loving mothers losing their kids to death or to the authorities and a common denominator - the repeated incident of forgetting the kids. The one quoted above was just one of them.

'Remember' is not a word that should ordinarily be used in the same sentence with a God who knows all things at every time. To really get the gist of this chapter we will have to explore this word especially what it means when it is associated with the supposedly all-knowing God. What does the Bible mean when it says, *God remembers?*

'But God remembered Noah and all the wild animals and the livestock that were with him in the ark, and he sent a wind over the earth, and the waters receded'.[2]

In the previous chapter, we saw through the life of Jesus and other examples that God can be trusted. We also established that lapses in memory are as a result of the fallen nature of man. God does not possess this nature and so He cannot forget things. He is described as omniscient; He knows all things. All things are open before Him, past, present and future. Still, there are passages in the Bible that make reference to God remembering things, people, issues etc. How do we reconcile these passages to the other passages that state that God does not forget? It is important to consider this issue because it touches on God's character and ability. There is no room for contradictions in God, He is either straightforward and we believe Him or confusing and by implication ceases to be the perfect One.

The first time the English Bible associated the word 'remember' with God was in Noah's case quoted above. For those of us who speak the English language, we must understand that the Bible was not originally written in our language and that though widely spoken; the English language is limited in expressing certain concepts. I know this first hand as a speaker of the Yoruba language. The Oxford English Dictionary defines the word 'remember' as follows:

> 1.   Retain in the memory, not forget, recall to mind, recollect, know by heart.

2.   Make present to

3.   Mention in prayer

4.   Convey greetings.

Applying the dictionary meaning of the word *remember* to what we know of God in the Bible, we can then say that in remembering us, God <u>retains us in His memory</u>. To recollect or recall means to bring something back that was for a time not in mind or at a place (in this case, God's mind), again from what we know of God's abilities, these words do not do justice to God's omnipotence. In remembering us, God retains us in His memory. Therefore, God remembering does not mean that He at any time did not have us in His memory.

The implications of God retaining us in His memory are numerous. We are constantly and permanently resident in His mind. He is constantly thinking about us.

We are talking about a God with whom nothing is difficult. Sadly, many of us are of the opinion in one way or the other that there are times when God does not think about us. *"Oh yea, He knows me, but at this moment, He has got other things on His mind"* we might think. Whilst thoughts like these can be excused because of our ignorance, they are actually an assault on God's integrity and might. God does not forget you!

Again delving deeper into the issue, if God cannot forget, what then did the Bible mean when it said "and God remembered Noah" (KJV)? As explained previously, Noah was on God's mind all the while, so the statement quoted above does not mean that God suddenly had a jolt of memory and *remembered* Noah who he had prior to that time forgotten. The Contemporary English Version of the Bible offers some help in understanding this:

> God did not forget about
> Noah and the animals with
> him in the boat. So God
> made a wind blow, and the
> water started going down.

God did not forget about Noah and the inhabitants of the ship. They were on His mind all along. The verse in question is not a standalone scripture but part of a story. Having a clear understanding of the context of the story will aid our understanding. The verse finishes with *So God made a wind blow, and the water started going down*. To further understand the passage, we must consider the **event** in question here; God made the waters recede. He performed <u>an act in time</u>, a definite act that happened at an appointed time (one of the many 40 day acts of God in the Bible).

This was something that God was going to do at the appointed time. So all the time that Noah, his family and the animals were in the ship, God was waiting for the time He had set when He would let them out. He did not forget them; He was simply waiting for the appointed time. 'And God remembered Noah' and God intervened in Noah's situation regarding the matter whose time had come.

With God and Noah, it was about timing. He was not going to make the waters recede until the time He had set for it. The human mind might think that God forgot Noah or was busy with some other things at the time and so Noah was not on His mind. But this was not the case.

There is a limit to my ability to multi-tasking and to what I can remember. As rightly observed by my Line Manager at a former workplace, I tend to forget things easily. What I did to help myself remember was to have a to-do-list of my duties and tick them as I went along in the day. By noon, I would probably have forgotten the first case I treated and if I had given any client an appointment, they had better pray that I had made a note of it in my planner. My primary duty at work was to attend to these clients and consider their cases. But more often than not, I did not give them any thought until my planner reminded me that I would be seeing them in a few moments.

But that is not how God operates, He is always thinking about us. Even if our set time for an issue has not come, we can have the confidence that His eyes are on us. The Protector of Israel does not doze or get drowsy.

Our problem is in thinking of God in human terms - but that is the only way we can think of Him! We have not seen the Father to verify if He has hands on which to tattoo our names. But that is how He describes Himself to us. In view of the fact that God uses human expressions in describing Himself, it is therefore easy for us to (wrongly) view Him as being human and attribute all human characteristics (including our weaknesses) to Him.

With us humans, 'remember' is the opposite of 'forget'. With God, remember is: 'the set time for this and that has now come, so let's get to work.' If at the moment things are not working for you and you think (like I do at times) that God has probably forgotten about you, remember that He is not like us and He does not forget.

If we must be honest with ourselves, don't we think that God forgets us because we do the same to Him? We forget Him! Like Rev Dick Lewis the former Vicar of Christ Church, Watford rightly pointed out to me whilst reviewing this book, "many times we forget about God and walk away from Him. Then we get into trouble and cry that we are forgotten by God". The Reverend Gentleman did not know that what he said described me perfectly. God cannot forget us, even though we often forget about Him and don't give Him the place He deserves in our everyday life.

There are various reasons known and unknown to us why things might not turn out as we want, making us switch to the 'God has forgotten me' mode. They include but are not limited to: God's timing, our asking and expecting things that are not in God's will for us, satan tampering with us, our sins etc. But whatever it is, it does not include God having a lapse of memory. Removing this from our list of options will help us to properly evaluate things and know where to channel our prayers and energy as required.

Before we move to the next chapter, we will consider another case of God 'remembering'.

> *'So when God destroyed the*
> *cities of the plain, he*
> *remembered Abraham, and*
> *he brought Lot out of the*
> *catastrophe that overthrew*
> *the cities where Lot had*
> *lived.'*[3]

Again, to understand this passage, we need to look into what happened previously. In Genesis 18:17-33, God informs Abraham of His decision to destroy Sodom and Gomorrah. Abraham pleaded with God to spare the cities if He could find ten righteous people in it. God agreed, but unfortunately the only people who God considered righteous in the city were just four in number - Lot, his wife and two daughters. The cities then had to be destroyed and their inhabitants killed. Two Angels were given the task of seeing to the execution of God's plan for the city. As they were about to commence operations, God *remembered* Abraham's request and spared Lot and his family.

The use of the word 'remember' here does not mean that God forgot His discussion with Abraham and then suddenly remembered it later. It was on God's mind all along. But no action was taken because the time for it had not come. Later God acted on His discussion with Abraham and spared

Lot and his ladies. Again I think that the issue here is of timing, God's timing.

In our everyday life, we all have the tendency to believe that there are moments when we are not on God's mind. His Word tells us that we are always on His mind, but we also need to understand that He will not act until the time is ripe for it. Ironically, our timing and God's are not always in sync. The challenge before us is to believe what God says and wait for it because it will come. And when it does, it will come in glory and honour. God makes everything beautiful in His time.

The Amplified Bible describes the passage in a very beautiful way:

'When God ravaged and destroyed the cities of the plain [of Siddim], He [earnestly] remembered Abraham **[imprinted and fixed him indelibly on His mind]**, and He sent Lot out of the midst of the overthrow when He overthrew the cities where Lot lived.'[4]   Emphasis added.

God imprinted and fixed him (Abraham) indelibly on His mind. Imprinting Abraham on His mind sounds to me like God tattooed Abraham on His mind. The indelible fixing also bears consonance with Abraham constantly being on God's mind. In the middle of the destruction of the cities, God had His conversation with Abraham on His mind. He did not forget it!

We can rejoice because God has fixed us on His mind! In health and sickness, ease and difficulty, holiness and sin, God is thinking about us and working in us for His good. His gaze is focused on us. It might be dry now, but God is in control and will see us through the drought. At the right time, we will come to the place He has prepared for us. God has not forgotten you; He is at work in your life. Poor Ms Rodriguez from our earlier story only remembered that her son was in the car when it was too late; God however has you in mind every second of the day. He that watches over Israel (replace Israel with your name) neither slumbers nor sleeps. Hallelujah!

RECAP

- We are always on God's mind

- God does not forget His own

- God has fixed times for the events in our lives and He works according to His timing

- At the right time, God will bring the answer to your prayers and fulfil His promises

- God cannot forget you, you can trust Him.

REFERENCES

1. http://www.dailymail.co.uk/news/article-2192989/Baby-dies-mother-forgets-car-hours-140F-temperatures.html

2. Genesis 8:1

3. Genesis 19:29

4. Psalms 121:4. Contemporary English Version

4.

GOD IS WORKING IT OUT

I believe God is managing affairs and that He doesn't need any advice from me. With God in charge, I believe everything will work out for the best in the end. So what is there to worry about?
- Henry Ford

Kids love puppets; as a child, I was intrigued by them. A good puppeteer pulls the strings and gets us all transfixed, carried away in a story to the wonderful world of Jingo and Maisy the squirrels that live in a little corner of squirrelly woods. Behind every puppet show are the people pulling the strings. Though not always visible to the audience, they control what happens on stage. There would be no puppet show without these folks. They are the alpha and the omega of the show, they call the shots.

I agree with William Shakespeare that *'all the world's a stage'* and stage manager is none other than God. There is nothing that happens to us that God does not know about. As a matter of fact, there is nothing that will ever happen to us that He does not have the foreknowledge of. God is omniscient, He knows all things. It becomes a little bit easier to understand this once you realise that the whole of time is contained in God.

Imagine everything, every aspect of your life, held in the being of God in an instant. Everything you have been, everything you are and everything you will be, there in the mind of God. He sees it all! He was at the beginning of time; He will be when time ceases to be. There is nothing He does not know about. I must be honest with you and confess that when I think of the sovereignty of God and how in His hands I am like a pawn, it makes me tremble. But I know I can trust Him with my life and that settles it (at least until I allow doubt to pervade my mind and I go over the process again).

We can go on and on about the almightiness of God and words will fail us. The picture I want you to have in your mind is that of this great Personality, this God being your Friend and Lover. A loving relationship is one of the most intimate of human relationships. When we love a person, we automatically place them above all else that exists in our world. We think about them, talk about them, spend time and do things with them. The whole of our world revolves around them and most importantly, we look out for them and give them our best. Likewise, God loves and gives you His best (His Son Jesus)[1] and as a true lover, He is looking out for you.

GOD'S SILENCE

In spite of the above mentioned, there are times when it seems as if God is absent from our lives, I refer to these as 'times of God's silence.' We experience them in various forms and at different times in life. They may be triggered by a variety of things; disaster, sickness, our sins, disappointment with life and everything we believe and so on. At such times our minds are troubled and we feel like we are alone in this world.

At a time like that in his life, David cried to God: 'my God, my God why have you forsaken me?'[2] This was a cry of desperation from a heart that felt forsaken and abandoned by God. If you have not had this sort of experience, you might not understand the gravity of it. But for those of us who have experienced it, we would rather be anywhere else than go back there. It is at times like these that our faith is put to test and we need the right friends around us to comfort us and speak faith-filled words to us.

I am a man of faith, but over the years I have gradually ceased to become a man of blind faith who takes in everything hook, line and sinker. I have become curious and intense in my search for spiritual understanding. I want to know the why and how of the things of God. For example, I want to know why Jesus came through Israel and not through the tribes resident in the British Isles, why He chose twelve men as disciples and not seven men and five women, knowing fully well that He was not a sexist leader. I want to engage my God-given senses in understanding my God-driven faith. And of course I want to understand what God was doing and where He was at the moments in my life when I felt forgotten. I want to know the answer to the question 'where is God when it hurts?'

Once again, we cannot crack this tough nut without having the background knowledge of God's character. He is righteous, unchanging and true. He does things in love; He gives in love, takes in love and withdraws Himself in love.

I use the language 'withdraws Himself' metaphorically, for God is ever present with us. Jesus told His disciples and us (His church), "And remember that I am always with you until the end of time"[3]. Paul said we survive in Jesus, "for in Him we live, move and have our being"[4]. David's most popular song, Psalms 23 ends with the words 'and I will dwell in the House of the Lord forever'. Jesus told His followers "Remain in me and I will remain in you"[5]. The scriptures tell us expressly that God through His Son Jesus is always with us. God is not in some far away planet looking down at us on earth. As His children, He lives in us and He has also positioned us with Him in the heavenly places. God is never absent!

It would have been deceitful for Jesus to say "I will be with you till the end of time" and then withdraw from us. Such an act would have made Him to be of the devil, the father of lies. But we see Jesus who lives in our hearts and at the same time sits beside God in heaven advocating for us. Therefore, as far as God is concerned, there is never a time that He leaves His children. People may desert us. They may promise to stand by us and then let us down. But 'God is true and every man a liar'[6].

God will not forsake you. He has committed himself in His Word. I like the song that came from Paul's heart when he thought about God's ever abiding presence with us:

Who shall separate us from
the love of Christ? Shall
trouble or hardship or
persecution or famine or
nakedness or danger or
sword? As it is written: "For
your sake we face death all
day long; we are considered
as sheep to be
slaughtered." No, in all
these things we are more
than conquerors through
him who loved us. For I am
convinced that neither
death nor life, neither
angels nor demons, neither
the present nor the future,
nor any powers, neither
height nor depth, nor
anything else in all creation,
will be able to separate us
from the love of God that is
in Christ Jesus our Lord.
Romans 8:35-39.

Nothing can make God stop loving you if you are
His chosen one. Your election was not of yourself,
He chose you before you knew Him. He chose you

because He wanted to, not because of anything you have done or will do. Your salvation is not of your own making, God sent Jesus to die for you whilst you were still sinning [7]. This is the highest form of love, God giving you His best and making you the best, for His name's sake.

Having established that the problem is not with God abandoning us, we shall proceed to look at some reasons for these dry spells in our lives. Chief amongst the things that we must understand is the issue of timing.

TIMING: 'There is a time for everything under the sun'[8]. A time to wake up at 6:30 PM in the morning – Mondays. A time to switch off the alarm and wake up at 10:00 AM - holidays.

God is orderly and as a master planner, He has marked out certain times in our lives as set times for certain things to happen. In ancient Greek, the word for this time is *Kairos*. It means time or season. **The right or opportune moment (the supreme moment).** God has an appointed time for every issue of our lives. He has set a time for you to be born, a time to go to school, get married, to start a business and so on. But don't be fooled into thinking that the right time for you is the same as everybody else's'. For example, if for some reasons you missed out of schooling as a child, it may well be that God has given you an opportunity to go back to school as an adult. God has our times marked out. Hear what Paul said about God's timing in his own life:

> But **when** God, who set me
> apart from birth and called
> me by his grace, **was**
> **pleased to reveal his Son in**
> **me** so that I might preach
> him among the Gentiles, I
> did not consult any man.
> Galatians 1:15-16 (Emphasis added)

Paul was a Pharisee, a very devout Jewish scholar. Out of zeal for God he saw to the imprisonment and execution of the group of Jews who claimed that Jesus was the Messiah, a heretical claim according to Paul's belief. It is of interest to me that Paul lived as a contemporary of Jesus but as far as we know, their paths did not cross whilst Jesus lived on earth. In Tarsus, Paul probably heard about the activities of a certain Jesus from Nazareth who was making waves in Galilee. I would have thought that considering the great feats that God would later use him for as a follower of Jesus, Paul would have been one of the twelve apostles.

But in God's timing, the *Kairos* for Paul's conversion was still some years ahead.

I submit that there are several *Kairos* in our lives, times marked out for specific events. In the process of waiting for *Kairos*, our hearts might grow weary and we think that God has forgotten us, but He has not. He is only waiting for the right time, the time planned ahead. Waiting time should not be time wasted, but a time of preparation for the manifestation of what is hoped for. In this time of his life, Paul took to studying; in her waiting time earlier in history, Sarah got busy going about her daily duties as the matriarch of Abraham's household and business. It is said that for four hundred years after God spoke through the prophet Malachi, He did not say anything again to anyone in Israel until an angel visited Zechariah and John the Baptist was born. The 400-year gap was a time for preparing the mind of Israel for the arrival of the Messiah. For even Jesus, God's Son had to come at His own *Kairos*, at the appointed time.

IMPATIENCE: We cannot talk about *Kairos* without mentioning patience. You need patience in order to possess what God has promised you. For example, if you feel an urge from God to start a school for children with mental disabilities say in the country of Togo, you need to wait on Him for further instructions on how, why and when (*Kairos*) He wants it done. Most times He might not tell you when or why, but He expects you to believe in Him and patiently start preparing yourself for the task as you wait for His next instruction.

Faith works with patience. I once heard Kenneth Copeland refer to them as the 'power twins'. The writer of the book of Hebrews links them up in this way:

> We do not want you to
> become lazy, but to imitate
> those who through <u>faith</u>
> <u>and patience</u> inherit what
> has been promised.
> Hebrews 6:12 KJV

The Message Bible expresses it beautifully thus: **'Don't drag your feet. Be like those who stay the course with committed faith and then get everything promised to them.'**

We need to be patient in our expectation of the fulfilment of God's promises. Impatience will make us think that God has forgotten us. It drives us to take steps outside God's will. It is not easy waiting on God for the fulfilment of a life goal, which remains delayed after you have done what you can to achieve it. But be rest assured that God too is waiting for the appointed time to arrive when He will bring to pass that good plan and expectation of yours. What then should you do to exercise patience at times like these?

- Understand that God is working in the background,

- Believe that at the right time, everything will work out well,

- Keep yourself busy in readiness for the moment that God has chosen for you. Get a job, go to school, re-train, have fun, be active in Church, volunteer for a charity, just do something good.

- Prepare yourself for the fulfilment of the promise God has made to you,

- Keep reminding yourself that your time will come. And it will definitely come.

SIN: Yes, the 's' word. God hates sin. Sin, be it rebellion against God or missing His mark for our lives blocks our ears from hearing God. The guilt sin brings dulls our conscience and our ability to receive from God, especially when we lead lifestyles that always disobey God.

But despite and even because of our rebellions and falling short of His holy standard often, God the loving Father reaches out to us. In Adam, sin created a deep gully between man and God. In Jesus we have a bridge builder. He is the bridge over the gorge. Through Him we get to God. When we sin and it looks like God has forsaken us, for it can really feel like that, we should take note of what John the beloved advised:

> If we say we have no sin [refusing to admit that we are sinners], we delude and lead ourselves astray, and the Truth [which the Gospel presents] is not in us [does not dwell in our hearts].
>
> If we [freely] admit that we have sinned and confess our sins, He is faithful and just (true to His own nature and promises) and will forgive our sins [dismiss our lawlessness] and [continuously] cleanse us from all unrighteousness [everything not in conformity to His will in purpose, thought, and action].
> 1 John 1:8-9. Amplified Bible.

When we sin, we should quickly run to God, repent and receive forgiveness. Please don't hide from God when you fall, He is longing to lift you up and set you on the path again. He knows that you will fall here and there. Our sins, whether big or small, pre-meditated or unintentional, are all well known to Him. His main care is that we put our faith in the saving power of Jesus and walk daily with Him. In your falling and rising up again, put your faith in Jesus. Without faith in God's Son, the continuous process of cleansing and forgiveness which God promises cannot be experienced. Our trust in the saving power of Jesus is the fuel for our sanctification.

SCANDALOUS LOVE – A Story of Forgiveness
If Jesus had told His story about a lost son today He might have said: 'the reckless son in his sin thought that Daddy had forgotten about him and had moved on. He could not pick the phone to call home. Guilt and shame would not allow him tell his colleagues in the pit his true identity. Unknown to him, Daddy had not had a minute rest since he left. Every day, Dad would check his inbox, expecting emails from his son. Any vibration from the mobile phone woke Dad up from his sleep, 'that might be my son calling' he would say. This went on and on until unable to contain himself, Dad converted the

living room out-looking the front garden into his bedroom. The staff thought it was a gimmick by the boss to monitor their punctuality. None of them knew it was a move by a Father who earnestly wanted to be the first to welcome his long lost son back into the compound and into the family. For even though he broke his Father's heart by his stupidity and wickedness, the Father's heart never for one moment left his son'.[9]

In our sins, we are like the reckless son, cut off (on our side) from our Father's love by our own deeds. But like the prodigal son's father, God's hands of love reach out to us and His 'mobile phone' is never switched off so that our call can come through. He has informed His staff to let us in anytime we show up. In another story, Jesus painted a picture of our Father God actively going out of His way to look for us. His is the love that transcends all love. He wants us more than we want Him. And when sin's stains soil us He invites us to get washed down and continue our journey.

The Lord says,
"Come, let us talk about these things.
Though your sins are like scarlet,
they can be as white as snow.
Though your sins are deep red,
they can be white like wool. [10]

51

Your sins might block your ears from hearing God's voice, but His love for you can never be stopped by your sins.

UNBELIEF: Without faith, it is impossible to please God[11]. Unbelief is a sin. In fact, it is one of the greatest sins we can commit against God. We question His character whenever we doubt Him. The Bible says a doubting man cannot receive anything from God. God does not take unbelief lightly. He wants us to have a firm belief in Him. Whoever trusts in Him will not be put to shame. The difference between going to heaven and going to hell is belief. One person believes in Jesus and is saved, another does not and he bound for hell - simple [12].

When we do not believe God or when we doubt His Word, we cut ourselves off from His provision; God's Word will not work in our lives if we don't believe it. Having said that, I must also say that there are times when in His Sovereignty He overlooks our unbelief and does whatever He wishes to do, but that does not stop the fact that God wants us to believe Him.

Still on the disadvantage of unbelief, St Paul explains that to fall from grace is to stop believing in Jesus as God's way of salvation. To disbelieve or adopt an attitude of unbelief towards Jesus and go back into thinking we can be saved by our good works or religion [13].

There are times when what we read in the Bible sounds incredible and simply impossible to the rational mind. But please don't dwell on the perceived impossibility; remember that with God all things are possible. A good example of what would constitute an impossible scenario for those of us living in the West is the issue of resurrection after death, the Bible records that Jesus raised Lazarus from the grave after three days[14]. To the scientific, rational western mind, this is impossible, but there have been countless reports of people who died and have been raised to life in our time.

If and when you have problems believing in God, tell Him in prayer. We all have issues with total reliance on God, but that should not stop us from approaching God and saying 'God, I am not sure if you exist at this moment, but if you do, please help me'. That is what Jesus refers to as a child-like faith in God and I tell you, He honours such faith. The gospel of Mark chapter 9 verse 24 records the story of the man who said to Jesus "Lord I believe - help my unbelief". When you seem not to feel or sense Him, don't let unbelief set in about Him. For that is the time to act in faith and trust your life to His unseen hands.

TOGETHER FOR GOOD

St Paul's thought that 'all things work together for good to them that love God' has been my anchor in trying times. I have come to realise that everything I go through will eventually be used by God for my benefit. My scars will become reference points for praise. My successes will culminate in me humbling myself in praise before Him who gives and takes away. God is at the helm of affairs and He will use everything you have gone through - your desert experience, the years you have gone without peace, the years that sin ate away, the times you felt that God had forsaken you - for your good. All these things are not beyond God's reach and I can assure you through His Word that they will turn out for your good. See what Paul wrote:

'And the Holy Spirit helps us
in our weakness. For
example, we don't know
what God wants us to pray
for. But the Holy Spirit prays
for us with groanings that
cannot be expressed in
words. And the Father who

knows all hearts knows
what the Spirit is saying, for
the Spirit pleads for us
believers in harmony with
God's own will. And we
know that God causes
everything to work together
for the good of those who
love God and are called
according to his purpose for
them. For God knew his
people in advance, and he
chose them to become like
his Son, so that his Son
would be the firstborn
among many brothers and
sisters.'[15]

As long as you keep your faith in Christ and love Him, everything you have experienced will become like ingredients in God's big pot of soup. And when God cooks, you had better bring your biggest plate and invite your friends to come share in the most delicious broth ever made.

Before we conclude this chapter, let's quickly touch on our human feelings and how God perceives us. God's Word clearly states that we are the apple of

His eyes and that we are engraved in the palms of His hands. As far as God is concerned, we are always in His sight, even if as human beings our situation and most especially our feelings suggest otherwise. I need to feel loved to know that I am loved, but my feelings can be highly deceptive. What really matters are acts of love from a lover, and not the goosebumps I get when I think of the concept of love.

Our feelings can be misleading especially when it comes to spiritual things. Again, we have to believe God because of His holy character and acknowledge that even if we don't 'feel' Him, He is still with us.

If the storm rages wildly and the boat about to break; if disease eats deep into our bones and our heart fails us for fear of the unknown; God remains in control and with time, our bodies and circumstances will respond to His mighty command of peace; be still!

RECAP

- God is in charge of our lives

- He is always in love with us

- There are times we feel He has forgotten us

- Several things are responsible for this, they include but are not limited to:

  Divine Timing: God moves at appointed times

  Impatience: We cannot outrun God; we need to wait on Him and for Him

  Sin: Our iniquities dull our senses to God's love.

  Unbelief: without faith, we cannot please God, God frowns on unbelief

- Everything that we have suffered and are still suffering will eventually be used by God for our good

- Regardless of what you feel, God is with you.

The Holy Spirit is praying for you, be at peace, you are not forgotten.

REFERENCES:

1. John 3:18

2. Psalms 22:1

3. Matthew 28:30. GOD'S WORD Translation

4. Acts 17:28

5. John 15:14

6. Romans 3:4

7. Romans 5:8

8. Ecclesiastes 3

9. Luke 15: 11-32

10. Isaiah 1:18. New Century Version

11. Hebrews 11:6

12. John 3:17-18

13. Galatians 5:4

14. John 11:43

15. Romans 8:26-29. New Living Translation.

5.

THE LAST LAUGH

God moves in a mysterious way His wonders to perform.

- William Cowper

The first line of the famous hymn quoted above is as true today as it was when it was first written.

'He who laughs last laughs best'! Nobody laughs who thinks that God has forgotten them. Laughter is mostly the physical response to pleasant information. I don't know about you, but for me the mere thought of being forgotten by those I hold dear is no laughing matter, let alone being forgotten by God. But because we know from scriptures that all things will come together for our good, we know that someday we shall laugh last. We shall laugh at all that we have been through. We shall laugh at the devil. We shall laugh in victory, and what is more? God Himself will laugh with us.

The basis for this hope is the line of scripture that: 'We are assured and know that [God being a partner in their labour] all things work together and are [fitting into a plan] for good to and for

59

those who love God and are called according to [His] design and purpose'[1].

God is a partner in our labour. He was with me in the hell-hole of UK Immigration detention in 2010 (And I must say that the UK Home Office needs to review the inhuman treatment that detainees in her various Immigration detention centres are subjected to. The behaviour of some of the guards are a slap on the integrity of this great nation).

Because God is always present with us in all our circumstances and struggles, we know that all things are working together and fitting into a plan - His plan. God has a good plan for you and when in His wisdom He leads you through tough times, it is also part of the plan for your welfare. In the end everything will be just right. Let's consider three points from the quotation in Romans 8:25 above.

GOD'S DESIGN AND PURPOSE ARE TO OUR ADVANTAGE

As established earlier in this book, God existed before man did and He created us. According to King David, our lives are mapped out before God; we are invited to play out the script He has written. He has a plan for us. Everything we have gone through, are experiencing and everything we will experience are all parts of that plan. The good news is that the plans of God are plans of 'good and not evil, to give us a future and a hope'.[2]

God's plan for you is good. A good God cannot have a bad plan; evil is not in God's character. Let's settle it once and for all that what we might perceive as an evil which God allows, is going to come out as good at the end of the day. It might not appear so at the moment, but we are told that it is FITTING into a plan. The pieces of the puzzle are being put together, the bricks are being laid. The parts are being manufactured in different workshops, and when everything comes together and is assembled, the beauty of the masterpiece will be seen.

Pause for a minute, and look back at how some of the difficult things you went through have helped you to become a better person today or helped bring you into a better situation. My detention experience helped me to focus and plan my life in the right direction.

God's plans for you are not going to appear ready made. No! They will materialise in the circumstances of life, a little here and there until the perfect mosaic is formed from the broken pieces of your life's experiences. Nothing that you go through is beyond God, He knows what will happen and He allows them because through them He will be glorified and you will become a better person.

The sovereign God has a purpose for your life and whether you like it or not, your life WILL play out according to His plan. Humanists and those who deny that our free will is ultimately subject to God's bigger purpose might disagree with this, but the supremacy of God is such that He has marked out our ways for us long before we were born. Examples of this abound in God's Word, the Bible. Centuries before Israel was formed as a nation, God told Abraham that his descendants will be slaves in a foreign land for four hundred years[3]. Again in the scriptures we see an incident where God preferred Jacob over his brother Esau before the twins knew right from wrong[4]. He hardened Pharaoh's heart in the drama that ensued before the Hebrews' exodus from Egypt. He used non Jewish Cyrus for His purpose[5]. He allowed satan to enter Judas and not Peter or John[6], Jesus prayed for Peter and not Judas who we might argue needed it most[7]. And God determined those saved before their birth[8].

God's purposes and designs are being worked out daily in our planet and individual lives. This takes us back to the frightening concept of being pawns in the hand of God, but may I quickly add that although we are pawns, we are in the hands of a loving God. In our post-modern world, it is a struggle to accept the fact of an intervening God, but the truth of this is clearly expressed in a line of a Cretan poem quoted by Paul 'in Him we live, move and have our being'[9]. It does not make sense to say that my actions including my sins, shortcomings and the few good acts that I commit are all doing the bidding of a Holy God, but to my dismay the Bible seem to suggest just that. 'If that is the case', you might ask 'why then does God frown on and punish our sins?' Paul devotes a large part of his writing in Romans chapter 9 to this issue. He explains:

> What then shall we say? Is God unjust? Not at all! For he says to Moses, "I will have mercy on whom I have mercy, and I will have compassion on whom I have compassion." It does not, therefore, depend on man's desire or effort, but on God's mercy. For the Scripture says to Pharaoh: "I

raised you up for this very
purpose, that I might
display my power in you
and that my name might be
proclaimed in all the earth."
Therefore, God has mercy
on whom he wants to have
mercy, and he hardens
whom he wants to harden.
Romans 9: 14-18

The buck stops with God and He is accountable to no one. He has told those of us who have become His children by believing in Jesus Christ His son that He loves that we should be rest assured that we can **walk right up to him and get what he is so ready to give. Take the mercy, accept the help**[11]. I love that! God said He will have mercy on whomever He wills and later He asks us to walk right up to Him and take the mercy. We are the recipients of his mercy!!!

God is for us. God has prepared the way for us if we are committed to Christ. God's intentions towards us are to our advantage. The road before us might be perilous but because we have been chosen by Him, we will make it through to God. It will all come together for our good.

OUR PART OF THE BARGAIN.

- FAITH.

We have a role to play and what we need to do is simple. Just believe God's word and act in faith. Whatever God says will definitely come to pass, nothing can stop it, but He has linked it to our faith. Now there are times when God works in our lives despite our doubts, a good example of this is the story of Sarah's conception of Isaac. She did not believe what God said, but God ignored her unbelief and did what He was determined to do[12]. This example is one of the few exceptions to the requirement of human faith in receiving from God. To believe God is to trust Him that He is in charge of issues even when it seems He is not.

We are not asked to trust a God who has not been proven. We are asked to trust Him whose intervening power has changed countless lives all around us. We are asked to trust Him who loves us so much that He gave His life for us, the God who not only gave us His son but gives us everything good with Jesus Christ the Son. We are asked to trust the one who knows our frailties, yet loves and accepts us, we are asked to trust God the good.

Faith believes that God is able to do what He promises, it trusts Him. I love the word trust. Trust means: reliance on the integrity, strength, ability, surety, etc., of a person or thing; confidence[13]. In trusting God, we rely on His integrity - He cannot fail; His strength- nothing can weaken His hold on us; His ability- He can do all things; His surety - He paid the ultimate price to secure us. He took our sins on Himself on the cross. You can trust God with your life!

In asking us to have faith in Him or trust Him, God is not asking us to perform great feats. He is just saying, 'Hey Oyin, trust me. When in doubt, trust me enough to talk to me about your doubt. You may be up or down in your trust level but no matter what, just trust me.'

- PATIENCE

Faith does not work alone; it needs patience for balance [14]. God has made all things available to us, we receive them with faith. In addition to faith we need patience because God's timing of events in our lives are not always in sync with our timing, therefore we need to wait patiently. 'Argh!' I scream at the mention of the word patience. My nature is to want everything now! But to my disappointment life does not work that way. With or without my patience, God will do whatever He wants to do <u>at the time He wants to do it</u>. If I hurry away from Him, I will come back and meet Him at the spot He is supposed to be at that point in time. Consequently, in order not to give myself unnecessary headaches, I need to apply patience to my faith and keep myself busy whilst waiting for God's promises to me. The Bible says the vision or promise from God will come. If it tarries we are asked to wait for it, for it will come without fail at the appointed time[15]. If like me, waiting is not one of your strengths then please pray to God to give you the virtue, patience.

- OBEDIENCE FUELED BY FAITH

If God asks you to do anything, please obey Him in faith. James said in his general letter that: 'faith that does nothing is worth nothing'[16]. The authorised version puts it this way: 'faith without works is dead'. Our faith expresses itself in obedience to God. Doing what God asks us to do shows that we have faith in Him, for without faith we cannot obey the voice of the invisible God. No one gets it right the first time. Many of us rise and fall in our walk of obedience to God. Humanly speaking obedience to God does not come naturally to us. But He understands our struggles and will help us to get up again when we fall into disobedience. I believe that as we keep our focus on Jesus, we will gradually find obeying God something that we can do. It might not be easy, but God will equip us with the ability to obey Him. If today you constantly disobey God despite the fact that you love Him, please do not write yourself off keep trusting Him and you will find help.

AND FINALLY

God is making all things work together for your good. The good times and the bad times, the planned and the unplanned are working together for your advantage. Nothing catches God unawares and it is all coming together and melting into a beautiful sculpture, God's work of art and masterpiece- a perfect you.

There will be times on earth when you feel that God has forgotten you, times when He will allow you to walk through the hottest furnace and experience the deepest sea beds…. times when He will remove the comfort of your bed and replace it with thorns, thistles and very sharp nails! Rick Warren said the reason for times like these is for the maturing of our friendship with God.

*To mature your friendship, God will
test it with periods of seeming
separation – times when it feels as if
he has abandoned or forgotten you.
God feels a million miles away. St
John of the Cross referred to these
days of spiritual dryness, doubt, and
estrangement from God as "the
dark night of the soul." Henri
Nouwen called them "the ministry of
absence." A.W. Tozer called them
"the ministry of the night." Others
refer to "the winter of the heart."[17]*

Whenever you go through any of these periods, and you will! Please always remember these assuring words from God;

Can a mother forget the infant at
her breast,
walk away from the baby she bore?
But even if mothers forget,
I'd never forget you—never.
Look, I've written your names on the
backs of my hands.

You will laugh last because God can never forget you. Let us draw near to the throne of God's grace with boldness today and receive mercy and grace to help in our time of need.

RECAP

- God in His sovereignty has good plans for us

- He shows mercy to whomever He wills

- He has made mercy available to His Children

- Our Part is to TRUST HIM, have PATIENCE for the promises to manifest and OBEY Him in faith.

- Because we are in God's plan, we will have the last laugh.

- All things are working together for our good.

REFERENCES:

1.   Romans 8:28. Amplified Bible

2.   Jeremiah 29:11

3.   Genesis 15:13

4.   Romans 9:3

5.   Exodus 7:3-13 (Pharaoh), Isaiah 44:28, 45:1 (Cyrus)

6.   Luke 22:3

7.   Luke 22:31-32

8.   Romans 9:1

9.   Acts 17:28

10.   Hebrews 4:16. New International Version

11.   Hebrews 4:16. The Message

12.   Genesis 18:10-15, Genesis 21:1-3

13.   http://dictionary.reference.com/browse/trustE

14.   Hebrews 6:12, James 1:3

15.   Habakkuk 2:3

16.   James 2:20. New Century Version

17.   Page 108, The Purpose Driven Life, copyright 2002 by Rick Warren.

YOU CAN HAVE ETERNAL LIFE!

Do you desire to be saved? By that I mean do you want to be saved from the punishment which the Bible teaches is coming on satan and humans who do not believe in Jesus Christ?

We are all sinners and we regularly disobey God. Adam and Eve the first human beings were created beautiful and sinless by God. But God's enemy, satan influenced them to disobey God.

By obeying satan, Adam and Eve became his slaves and enemies of God. They became destined to suffer in the punishment that God had reserved for satan, a former angel who rebelled against God and was banished from heaven to the earth.

God prepared a place called hell and another called the lake of fire, both are large areas burning with fire and brimstone. These were prepared as everlasting punishment for satan and his other fallen angels. And because of our sins, humans too became shortlisted for this horrible place. The fires of hell don't burn out.

But because of His great love for us humans, his choice creation, God sent His Son Jesus Christ to suffer and die in our place. Adam and Eve sinned by obeying satan. They were destined to be eternally punished.

Jesus came to take upon Himself the punishment due to Adam and Eve and all of humanity. He lived in Israel for over 33 years helping people, healing the sick, preaching that people should turn from sinning and have a change of attitude. He urged people to turn to God. He was lied against by the authorities of His days and killed, executed on a roman cross like a common criminal.

However, in God's grand plan the death of Jesus was the sacrifice necessary to save the whole world. When Jesus died, the demand of justice was met. Adam's sin was paid for. Now man is totally free.

Three days after His execution, Jesus became alive again! Forty days afterwards, He ascended into Heaven. He is seated in Heaven today at God's right hand praying for you.

Now Jesus asks you to believe in Him as the Son of God and as the one who has taken your place in Hell.

He promised that when you do, you will have everlasting life. He said that when you die, you can be sure that you will go to heaven. A place of everlasting bliss where there is no more sorrow but joy that lasts forever.

Those who refuse to believe in Jesus after being told of the beautiful thing He has done are still under the condemnation of Adam's rebellion against God. Sadly, they will suffer in hell with satan after they die physically in this world.

Believe in Jesus today in your heart and pray to God in Jesus' name. Ask God to put His Holy Spirit in you. He surely will. As you believe in Jesus, God will wipe your sins away and make you a citizen of His Kingdom.

Please do that today and get in touch with me, I will help you to know more about God's wonderful gift of salvation to you- Jesus His Son.

For God so loved the world that he gave his one and only Son, that whoever believes in him shall not perish but have eternal life.

John 3:16

God loves you.

THANK YOU!

It takes a village to raise a child. It certainly took a village of minds to 'raise' this book.

My first thanks go to The Rev Canon Dick Lewis, the former Vicar of Christ Church Watford. When I informed him about this book, he enthusiastically volunteered to edit it. I owe the accuracy and theological balance of this book to Him. I must confess that some of the expressions here are actually his, word for word. I also thank Mrs Elizabeth Yaroson of Hornchurch, London for her further editorial work.

Thanks to the management of Hope Publications for their permission to publish this book under their auspices.

To all of who helped in one way or the other to contribute to the story in this book and to distribute it, I say a big thank you.

CONTACT THE AUTHOR

Email: oyinoladipo@gmail.com

Twitter: @oyinoladipo

Facebook: Oyin Oladipo

Skype: oyinlade.oladipo

Made in the USA
Charleston, SC
27 February 2017